Gr_____ch

# LEWIS AND CLARK'S CONTINENTAL JOURNEY

## Elizabeth Raum

Heinemann Library
Chicago, Illinois

Produced for Heinemann Library by
Monkey Puzzle Media Ltd

Picture Research by Lynda Lines
Designed by Jane Hawkins and Victoria Bevan

Originated by Modern Age
Printed and bound in China

12 11 10 09 08
10 9 8 7 6 5 4 3 2 1

**Library of Congress Cataloging-in-Publication Data**

Raum, Elizabeth.
 Lewis and Clark's continental journey / Elizabeth Raum.
  p. cm. -- (Great journeys across Earth)
 Includes bibliographical references and index.
 ISBN-13: 978-1-4034-9757-4 (hb) --
 ISBN-13: 978-1-4034-9765-9 (pb)
1. Lewis and Clark Expedition (1804-1806)--Juvenile literature. 2.
West (U.S.)--Discovery and exploration--Juvenile literature. 3. West
(U.S.)--Description and travel--Juvenile literature. 4. Lewis,
Meriwether, 1774-1809--Juvenile literature. 5. Clark, William,
1770-1838--Juvenile literature. 6. Explorers--West
(U.S.)--Biography--Juvenile literature. I. Title.
F592.7.R38 2007
917.804'2--dc22
                          2007005833

**Acknowledgments**
The author and publisher are grateful to the following for permission to reproduce copyright material: Bridgeman Art Library p. **38**; Corbis p. **15** (Bettmann), p. **22** (Macduff Everton), p. **25**, p. **26** (Blue Lantern Studio), p. **27**, p. **28**, p. **29** (Philip James Corwin), p. **36** (Bob Rowan/Progressive Image); Fort Clatsop National Memorial Collection p. **34–35**; Charles Fritz Fine Art p. **14**; Getty Images p. **6** (Hulton Archive), p. **10** (Hulton Archive), p. **13** (Jeff Foott), p. **21** (James Balog), p. **31** (Philip Schermeister/National Geographic); Mary Evans Picture Library p. **39**; Michael Haynes p. **5**, p. **40**; Gary R. Lucy Gallery p. **1**, p. **8**; Montana Historical Society p. **17** (Don Beatty); Nature Picture Library p. **20** (Thomas Lazar); NHPA p. **11** (Rich Kirchner); North Wind Picture Archives p. **41**; Still Pictures p. **9** (Jim Wark), p. **18–19** (Jim Wark), p. **24** (Bert Gildart); Topfoto p. **12**; U.S. Army Center of Military History p. **30**, p. **32**, p. **33**.

Maps by Martin Darlison at Encompass Graphics.

Cover photograph of bison in South Dakota reproduced with permission of FLPA (Mark Newman).

Title page picture of Lewis and Clark's men pushing their keelboat through the shallow water of the Missouri River reproduced with permission of Gary R. Lucy Gallery.

Expert read by Rob Bowden, geography and education consultant.

Every effort has been made to contact copyright holders of any material reproduced in this book. Any omissions will be rectified in subsequent printings if notice is given to the publisher.

The paper used to print this book comes from sustainable resources.

# Contents

Some words are shown in bold, **like this**. You can find out what they mean by looking in the glossary.

# Lands Unknown

In 1800 the western part of North America was as much a mystery as the Moon. Few people in the world knew what the land was like, or what kind of plants and animals lived there. It was a place that was waiting to be explored.

## A curious president

Thomas Jefferson was president of the United States from 1801 to 1809. He believed that woolly mammoths roamed the western countryside. He imagined a place dotted with erupting volcanoes, giant bears, and poisonous snakes. He believed that the Mandans, who were a Native American tribe living in the West, had wandered there from Wales (one of the four countries that make up the United Kingdom). Jefferson wanted to meet these people, whom he called "savages."

But Jefferson was president. He could not go off exploring. So, in 1802, he chose his personal assistant, Meriwether Lewis, to lead an expedition into the unknown lands. Lewis jumped at the chance to go.

## A trusty team

Lewis asked his old friend William Clark to lead the journey with him. When word went out that Lewis and Clark were organizing an expedition, volunteers rushed to sign up. Lewis and Clark chose loyal soldiers who knew how to survive in the wilderness. They called the expedition the **Corps** of Discovery.

### Meriwether Lewis (1774—1809)

*Meriwether Lewis grew up in Virginia. Thomas Jefferson was his family's neighbor. When Lewis was five years old, his father died during the **Revolutionary War**. As a boy Lewis fished and hunted. His mother taught him about **medicinal herbs**. At age 20 he joined the army and served on the **frontier**. In 1801 President Jefferson chose Lewis to be his assistant.*

### William Clark (1770–1838)

*Like Lewis, William Clark was born in Virginia. At age 14 he moved to the Kentucky frontier, where he learned how to survive in the wilderness. At 19 Clark joined the army. Lewis and Clark served together as soldiers for about six months in 1795. Clark was running the family farm in Kentucky when Lewis asked him to join the expedition.*

Captains Lewis and Clark visited army forts gathering volunteers to serve in the Corps of Discovery.

# Early Days

Jefferson and Lewis spent nearly two years preparing for the expedition. They studied maps of the West that had big, empty spaces between St. Louis, in Missouri, and the Pacific Ocean. They planned to fill in the map.

## Rivers for trade

Jefferson wanted Lewis to travel west along the Missouri River and find a water route across the continent. He believed that the Colorado or Columbia rivers connected the Missouri to the Pacific Ocean. Finding a river route across North America would encourage people to move west, set up **trading posts**, and send goods back and forth across the country. In the 1800s all heavy items or large shipments had to travel by boat. Roads did not exist in much of the country, and building them took time and money. Rivers provided the quickest and least expensive way to move heavy and large things from one place to another.

Thomas Jefferson (1743–1826), author of the Declaration of Independence, became the third president of the United States in 1801.

## The Louisiana Purchase

On April 30, 1803, President Jefferson purchased (bought) 828,000 square miles (more than 2 million square kilometers) of land in central North America. The land had been owned by France and was called the Louisiana **Territory**. It was renamed the Louisiana Purchase. This purchase meant that Lewis and Clark would not have to travel through land claimed by France.

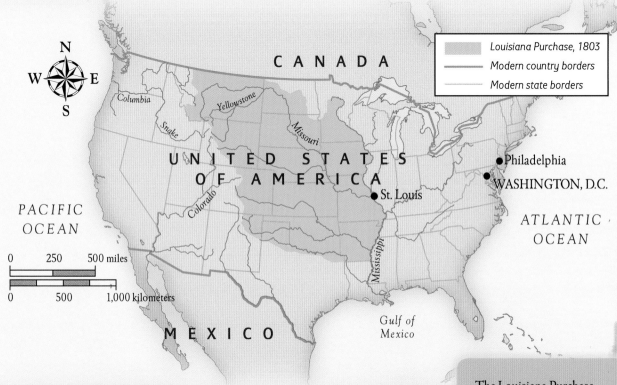

## Maps and records

Lewis and Clark would take boats on their journey, but they would have to explore the land around the rivers on foot.

Jefferson instructed the men to make maps and take notes about rivers, mountains, and other natural **landmarks**. He wanted to know about the weather. Was the land good for farming? What kind of wildlife lived in the West? He sent Lewis to Philadelphia to meet the best scientists of the day. They taught Lewis how to preserve plant and animal samples. A doctor named Benjamin Rush gave Lewis lessons on how to treat common illnesses and injuries.

The Louisiana Purchase doubled the size of the United States and cleared the way for exploration.

## Making provisions

During the summer of 1803, Lewis gathered supplies. He bought guns, **ammunition**, knives, and fishhooks. He ordered boxes of dried soup mix. A boat builder made a spare iron boat frame that came in two pieces. These could be put together and covered with animal hides, ready to float. Lewis also bought kettles, tents, uniforms, tools, tobacco, and gifts for Native Americans.

## Keelboat and pirogues

Lewis designed a **keelboat** that was 55 feet (nearly 17 meters) long and 8 feet (2.4 meters) wide in the middle. There was a small cabin on deck. The boat could be rowed, sailed, pushed, or pulled, depending on the state of the river. The expedition also took two **pirogues** (canoes), one white and one red.

Lewis and Clark's men often had to push their keelboat through shallow or clogged-up water using poles. Sometimes they pulled the boat through with ropes.

## Setting sail

The **corps** set sail on May 14, 1804. Clark guided their brand new keelboat up the muddy Missouri River. On May 25 they passed the last white **settlement**. By July 30 the corps had traveled 640 miles (1,030 kilometers).

Lewis walked along the river shore taking samples of plants and soil. He made detailed notes on unfamiliar plants and animals. Sometimes he and the other men made drawings. In early August Lewis killed a bull snake so that he could accurately describe it. He identified coyotes, white pelicans, pronghorn antelope, **prairie** dogs, and many species of fish that were new to science.

### The Big Muddy

*The Missouri River covers 2,315 miles (3,725 kilometers) from its source in present-day Montana to where it joins the Mississippi, near St. Louis, Missouri. The Missouri is known as "the big muddy" because fine sand and soil cloud its water. Today, the Missouri has far less water than it did in 1800, making it much narrower than it used to be. This is partly because many **dams** have now been built across the river.*

This photograph, taken in present-day Montana, shows how the Missouri River twists and turns as it winds its way south.

# Into the Prairies

As the **corps** struggled up the Missouri, they entered **prairie** country. In these huge, open grasslands, they saw many new plants and animals. They also met Native Americans for the first time.

## Records of the land

Lewis and Clark never forgot President Jefferson's orders to make maps and record their journey. Clark measured the land and the river as they traveled along it. During the expedition he made more than 140 separate maps. Each night, the men of the corps wrote in their journals about what they had seen that day. One of the men, Patrick Gass, drew pictures of events along the trail. These included the first meeting between Captain Lewis and Native Americans.

This drawing of captains Lewis and Clark meeting with Native Americans at Council Bluffs, Nebraska, is from the journal of Patrick Gass.

## Death and election

On August 20, 1804, a member of the expedition named Sergeant Floyd died, probably of **appendicitis**. Two days later the corps voted for Patrick Gass to take Floyd's position as a sergeant. Some historians consider this to be the first election held west of the Mississippi River.

## Life on the prairies

Lewis and Clark wrote of the lush grasses, the good soil, and the many unknown animals and plants they saw on the prairies. The prairies are North America's grasslands, also called the Great Plains. They reach from southern Canada to Texas. Clark noted in his journal that prairie grass is sweet and makes good animal feed. During the summer, natural prairie grasses can grow up to 12 feet (nearly 4 meters) tall.

Often the men saw fires on the prairies. Some of these started when lightning struck the long grasses during storms. Native Americans also lit fires, using the smoke to send signals from one tribe to another.

## First meeting

Lewis and Clark's first meeting with Native Americans went well. Lewis told the chiefs of the Oto and Missouri tribes that the United States wanted to trade with them. Then, Lewis gave gifts of tobacco, U.S. flags, and medals. The medals had Jefferson's face on one side and hands shaking in friendship on the other. Lewis' speech to the chiefs lasted an hour. It took another hour to translate it into the Native American languages.

On September 14, 1804, the expedition spotted pronghorn antelope. Among the fastest animals in the world, they were unknown to scientists before the expedition.

## Lost along the way

On August 26 the captains sent George Shannon, the youngest member of the expedition, to find two horses that had wandered away from camp. Shannon found the horses, but got lost on his way back. He traveled north along the river, hoping to find the expedition ahead. When he finally realized that they were behind him, he stopped and waited for the others to catch up. With no maps and no way to communicate, getting lost was a constant danger.

## Meeting the Yankton Sioux

One of the most trusted men of the corps was Sergeant Nathaniel Pryor. He was the first to visit a Yankton Sioux camp. The Yanktons were friendly. They mistook Pryor for the expedition's leader and tried to carry him into their camp. They cooked a fat dog and invited Pryor to join the feast.

Later, Lewis and Clark arrived. Lewis gave a speech about peace, and the Yanktons showed the corps their skills with bows and arrows. They celebrated well into the night, dancing to the music of deer-hoof rattles and a drum.

This 1890 painting shows a Sioux dance. The dancer closest to the fire wears a buffalo headdress.

## The Sioux

The "Sioux" tribes Lewis and Clark wrote about are more properly called the Dakota, Lakota, or Nakota peoples. The Sioux, including the Yanktons, depended on bison for food, shelter, and clothing. They lived in tepees (tents) made of bison hides, which they could move from place to place.

This picture shows a herd of American bison. Native Americans hunted bison for meat. They used the fur for blankets and the hides to build their tepees.

### American bison

*American bison, also known as American buffalo, are giant wild cattle. They travel in groups called herds. As many as 60 million roamed the plains in 1804. In the late 1800s railroad companies hired hunters to kill off the bison. They believed that killing them would force the Native Americans to leave the prairies in search of other food. Today, only about 300,000 bison survive.*

## Dangerous pests

The journals of Lewis and Clark are filled with complaints about mosquitoes. Mosquito bites were annoying and dangerous. Malaria, a disease spread by mosquitoes, was common in the United States in the 19th century. Symptoms include chills and fever. Victims suffer from headaches, vomiting, and weakness. Malaria can last for months and kill. Today, there are medicines that lessen the risk of catching malaria, but it is still a serious problem in Africa and Asia.

## September change

The corps welcomed September because the cooler temperatures meant there were fewer mosquitoes. Prairie grasses turned golden, and there were plenty of fat deer and antelope for the men to hunt and eat. But Lewis and Clark were nervous about meeting the Teton Sioux, a powerful tribe that controlled the Missouri River.

The Teton Sioux were celebrating a victory over their enemies, the Omaha, when Lewis and Clark entered the village.

## Trouble trading

The Teton Sioux expected all who passed by their villages to trade with them. Lewis and Clark offered some cheap gifts. But the Teton Sioux were used to French and British fur traders, who brought with them tobacco and gunpowder. Lewis and Clark refused to give more because they believed that a Teton Sioux warrior had stolen an expedition horse.

### Trading gifts

*The corps took gifts to buy horses, food, canoes, and help from Native Americans along the way. They included:*

 5 lbs (2.3 kg) white glass beads

 288 common brass thimbles

 10 lbs (4.5 kg) sewing thread, assorted

 50 lbs (23 kg) spun tobacco

 24 blankets

 36 ear trinkets

European fur traders often bought furs from Native Americans in exchange for tobacco, guns, and other items.

# Winter with the Mandan

On October 24, 1804, the expedition reached two Mandan villages. These were busy trading centers, where Native Americans and white visitors exchanged goods. The Mandan people welcomed the **corps** to stay for the winter.

It took the corps over five months to travel the 1,600 miles (2,575 kilometers) from St. Louis to the Mandan villages.

## Talk at the camp

As they set up camp, Lewis and Clark communicated with the local Mandan and Hidatsa people. The explorers wanted to find out all they could about the country that lay to the west. Tribal leaders told Lewis and Clark that the Shoshone, who lived in the mountains to the west, could sell them horses for the journey.

Every day, Mandan villagers stopped by the expedition's camp. In early November a French trader named Charbonneau visited. He brought along his pregnant wife, Sacagawea, who was Shoshone.

Historians believe that Sacagawea was kidnapped by the Hidatsa when she was about 12 years old and brought to the Mandan villages. Later, Charbonneau, a French fur trader, bought her to be his wife. Sacagawea became one of the most valuable members of the expedition.

## Communication

Charbonneau offered his services as translator. The captains agreed. They hoped that Sacagawea would be able to speak to the Shoshone, her native tribe.

Lewis and Clark depended on translators when they spoke with Native Americans. This usually involved a long chain of conversation. For example, Sacagawea would speak Hidatsa to Charbonneau; he translated that into French; then Drouillard, a French-speaking member of the corps, translated those words into English. It was little wonder that sometimes the original meaning was lost along the way!

### A slave named York

*Traveling with the expedition was an African-American man named York. York was one of many slaves owned by Clark's family. Slavery was legal in the United States until 1865. York went everywhere with Clark. After the expedition, he asked for his freedom. Clark refused until sometime after 1811. In 1815 Clark gave York a wagon and team so that he could earn a living by running a carting business.*

Sacagawea, a Shoshone woman, and York, a slave, were valued members of the Corps of Discovery.

## The winter freeze

As winter approached, Lewis and Clark's men were shocked by the extreme cold. They continued to go out hunting, but on December 8 Clark noted in his journal that several of the men returned with **frostbite**. Clark measured the temperature with his thermometer—it was well below freezing, at -12°F (-24°C).

### Extreme climate
*Lewis and Clark wrote about the freezing temperatures during the winter of 1804–05. Present-day North Dakota, where the Mandan villages were located, has a **continental climate**. This means it has extremes of temperature during the year. It can be as hot as 90°F (32°C) or more in summer, then dip to -20°F (-29°C) or colder in winter.*

In late December 1804 the men completed their base and named it Fort Mandan. The captains kept the men busy despite the chilling weather. In addition to hunting, they completed military exercises, stood guard, sewed buckskin clothing, cleaned equipment, and prepared food. Corps member Pierre Cruzatte often played his fiddle. On New Year's Day a Mandan chief invited him to play for the holiday party. Everyone danced to drums, rattles, and the fiddle. Celebrations continued until January 5, with dancing, talking, and eating. The explorers enjoyed Mandan corn and dried bison meat.

## A new baby

On February 11, 1805, Sacagawea gave birth to a son. She named him Jean Baptiste Charbonneau. Captain Lewis was present at the birth. He wrote that the baby was a "fine boy." Jean Baptiste, whom Clark nicknamed "Pomp," became the youngest member of the expedition.

The corps built Fort Mandan on the banks of the Missouri. This full-size model of the fort was constructed in 1971.

### A big population
*When Lewis and Clark arrived in present-day North Dakota, the Mandan villages and nearby Hidatsa towns included about 4,000 people. This was more than the population of Washington, D.C., which at the time was called Washington City. In those days just 3,210 people lived in the capital city. Today, about 551,000 people live there.*

# Mission to the Falls

In April, with the arrival of spring, it was time to move on from Fort Mandan. The Hidatsa people had told the **corps** there was a waterfall further along the Missouri. The captains were determined to find it.

## Packages for home

Before they left, Lewis and Clark sent several men back to St. Louis in the **keelboat**. They packed it full of letters to family, notes, scientific drawings, plant, animal, and rock samples, and gifts from Native Americans. They sent a live **prairie** dog, a prairie hen, and four magpies. Clark included a map he had drawn.

## Back on the river

On April 7, 1805, the rest of the corps headed west in six small canoes and the red and white **pirogues**. At first the trip was easy and there were plenty of animals to hunt for food. The corps shot deer, bison, antelope, and bear. On May 19 Lewis' dog, Seaman, was attacked by a beaver. The cut was deep, but Seaman recovered.

On June 3 the corps arrived at a fork (split) in the Missouri River. Lewis and Clark studied the two rivers. Either one could be the Missouri. They decided to split up and explore the area. When they met back at the fork a few days later, the captains were convinced that the southern fork was the right one.

Lewis and Clark named prairie dogs "barking squirrels" because of their cry.

### Meat for the journey

*Lewis and Clark lived off the land. One expert estimated that the expedition killed and ate 1,001 deer, 375 elk, 227 bison, 62 pronghorn, 35 bighorn sheep, 43 grizzly bears, 23 black bears, 113 beavers, 16 otters, 104 geese, 45 ducks, 46 grouse, 9 turkeys, 48 plovers, and 1 wolf. They also ate 190 dogs and 12 horses.*

### Grizzly bears

*Of all the animals the corps encountered, grizzly bears were the most dangerous. Adult grizzlies can be enormous, the heaviest weighing up to 1,700 pounds (630 kilograms). Grizzly bears, also called brown bears, are **omnivores**. This means they eat both plants and other animals. But when these foods run short, they may attack humans.*

Grizzly bears posed a serious danger to the corps. Several times the men climbed trees to escape hungry bears.

## Problems at the Falls

Lewis led a small group overland in search of the Great Falls, leaving Clark and the rest on the river with the boats. Lewis heard the Great Falls before he saw them. When he reached the waterfall around noon on June 13, he called it "the grandest sight I ever beheld." Lewis discovered five waterfalls and at least 5 miles (8 kilometers) of rapids. Sailing the river would be impossible.

Lewis headed back to camp. On his way, a grizzly chased him. He jumped into the river, and the bear turned away. Next, he saw what he thought was a wolf, but he later decided it was a "tyger cat" (probably a lynx). Several yards further, three bison bulls charged at him. The next morning Lewis found a rattlesnake curled up near where he slept. He must have been relieved to rejoin the others!

Lewis described the Great Falls in his journal and wrote that they were "truly magnificent."

## Passing the Falls

At the Great Falls, the Missouri River drops 512 feet (156 meters) in less than 10 miles (16 kilometers). Melting snow flows into the river every spring, making it especially full and dangerous. When Lewis and Clark arrived, the river was at its highest after summer rains.

The corps built two big wagons to carry, or **portage**, their supplies around the Great Falls. Bears, rattlesnakes, and mosquitoes tormented them. They also suffered from fierce heat and storms. Rough ground and prickly plants wore out the men's shoes every two days. They had to stop and make new ones from animal skins. It took a month to pass the falls and rebuild boats and supplies.

The portage around the Great Falls (shown in the inset map below) was one of the most difficult parts of the journey.

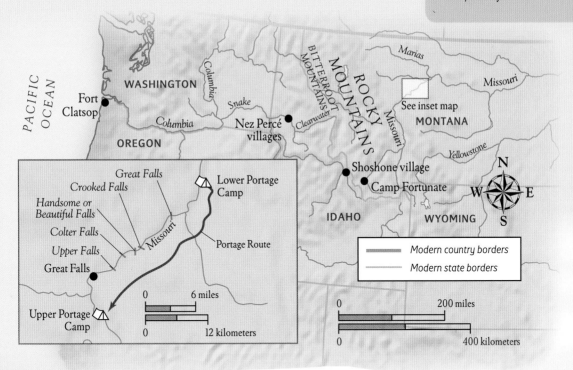

### Prickly pears
Lewis called mosquitoes, gnats, and prickly pears the expedition's "trio of pests." The prickly pear is a flowering cactus that grows from southern Canada to Mexico. The flowers are usually red, pink, yellow, or purple. Prickly pears spread low on the ground and can be a hazard underfoot, as the men of the corps discovered.

# Into the Mountains

Lewis and Clark were eager to find the Shoshone people, who they knew could sell them fresh horses. On July 22, 1805, Sacagawea recognized the land where she had lived as a child. This was Shoshone country.

## A rocky divide

The strange thing was, there were no Shoshone. In mid-August, Lewis went searching. He followed a horse trail into the mountains, which took him to a small stream. The stream fed water into the mighty Missouri River. Lewis took a drink, rested briefly, then continued his climb. He came to a ridge. The streams on one side of the ridge flowed east. On the other, they flowed west. Lewis had reached the **Continental Divide**.

As the corps crossed the mountains of the upper Missouri River, they saw bighorn sheep.

When Lewis looked west, he saw the tall, rocky peaks of the Bitterroot Mountains. But he could not see a river. The truth hit Lewis hard. There was no way of passing the mountains by boat. They would have to climb across on foot or, if they were lucky, on Shoshone horses.

## Chief Cameahwait

On August 13 Lewis and his men met a group of 60 Shoshone warriors. The chief, Cameahwait, welcomed Lewis to his camp. Lewis smoked a **peace pipe** with Cameahwait. Clark and the rest of the **corps** were still struggling up the river. When they also arrived at the camp a few days later, a Shoshone woman ran up to Sacagawea and hugged her. It was an old friend. Sacagawea jumped for joy.

A few moments later, Sacagawea recognized Cameahwait. He was her brother! She ran to him. Lewis and Clark named the place Camp Fortunate.

**Speaking Shoshone**

*Lewis and Clark expected Sacagawea to translate Shoshone. Few people speak this language today. In fact, the Shoshone language was not a written language until the late 1970s. Today, Shoshone leaders are trying to save their language. Below are some common Shoshone words:*

*horse—bungu*
*bear—weda'*
*bison—bozheena*
*dog—sadee'*
*snake—basimu'yu*

This Umatilla chief from eastern Oregon is shown holding a peace pipe similar to the one Lewis smoked with Cameahwait.

## Hunger in the mountains

The corps and the Shoshones remained at Camp Fortunate for several days. The captains took turns exploring the region. They bought 29 horses from the tribe. One old Shoshone man, whom Lewis and Clark called Old Toby, agreed to guide the expedition over the mountains.

In the Bitterroots, winter was setting in. Travel was slow and dangerous. Clark noted that everywhere he looked there were more mountains to cross. On September 3, 1805, it snowed. Hunters came back empty-handed, so the captains had three colts (young male horses) killed for food. The men were so hungry they ate their candles. Eleven days after entering the mountains, they stumbled out "more dead than alive."

This 1920 drawing shows the corps struggling through the mountains with the help of Old Toby.

## Bitterroot Mountains

*The Bitterroot Mountains (sometimes called the Bitterroot Range) run along the Montana–Idaho state border. They extend for 365 miles (588 kilometers) and reach a height of 11,393 feet (3,475 meters). Winter begins early in the Bitterroots—the corps found snow there in late August. The Bitterroots are part of the great Rocky Mountains (see page 36).*

This 1877 photo shows a Nez Percé chief named Looking Glass sitting on his horse in front of a tepee.

## Kindness to strangers

On September 20, 1805, the corps came out of the mountains. Soon the group arrived at a village led by Chief Twisted Hair of the Nez Percé tribe, on a branch of the Clearwater River. Twisted Hair welcomed everyone and offered them lily roots and fish to eat.

Meanwhile, Twisted Hair debated what to do. If he killed the explorers and took their weapons and trade goods, his people would be the richest in the West. But a woman named Watkuweis stepped forward and defended the explorers. She told Twisted Hair that a white man had treated her well when the Blackfeet (see page 38) had captured her seven years earlier. The corps were safe.

## Naming places

Lewis and Clark made up names for the places they visited. They named many after themselves ("The Lewis and Clark River"), friends and family ("Judith's River"—after Clark's cousin Judith Hancock), or after events ("Colt Killed Creek," where the corps killed a colt for meat). Most places already had Native American names. Many were called different things later.

## Sick of salmon

At the Nez Percé camp, the corps suffered strange stomach cramps and vomiting. A sudden change of diet may have caused this sickness, or perhaps the salmon they ate contained unfamiliar **bacteria**. It was more than a week before the men were well enough to leave. As they recovered, they made canoes to sail downriver.

Twisted Hair traveled with the corps down the Clearwater. They had to dodge rapids in their dugout canoes. It was a dangerous journey. On October 10 the men canoed into a new river—the Snake. Here, there were plenty of salmon, but the men wanted meat. They bought dogs from local natives to kill for food. Clark noted in his journal that most of the men seemed to enjoy eating dog. He did not.

### Salmon

*At the time the corps were traveling, about 16 million salmon swam in the Columbia and Snake rivers. Environmentalists estimate that today there are less than 1 percent of that number—no more than 160,000.* **Dams** *on the river (see opposite) and* **pollution** *have killed many river animals, including the salmon.*

This 1911 photo shows a Native American fisherman spearing salmon in the Columbia River.

## Waters new

Native Americans along the river were friendly, partly because Twisted Hair was with the corps. Lewis and Clark carefully noted how each tribe looked, behaved, and spoke. They met Yakimas, Wanapams, Wallawallas, and others.

On October 15 the corps reached the Columbia River. They were the first white men to travel that section of water. They camped for two days while Clark explored the area.

The Bonneville Dam spans the Columbia River between the states of Oregon and Washington.

### The Columbia River
*The Columbia begins in present-day British Columbia, Canada. From there it flows southwest through Washington state toward the Pacific Ocean. The river is 1,214 miles (1,954 kilometers) long. Dams have been built at various points along it, equipped with machinery that produces **hydroelectric power**.*

# In Search of the Coast

Soon the **corps** were racing down the Columbia River. They made good progress, but there were hazards still to come. On October 23 the group reached the first of several waterfalls.

## Rough water

Rushing rapids and rocky cliffs made this section of river very dangerous. The captains hired local people to help carry supplies around the falls, while the corps sailed through the rapids whenever they could. At one steep drop the men sent their canoes over the falls empty, then hiked down to collect them.

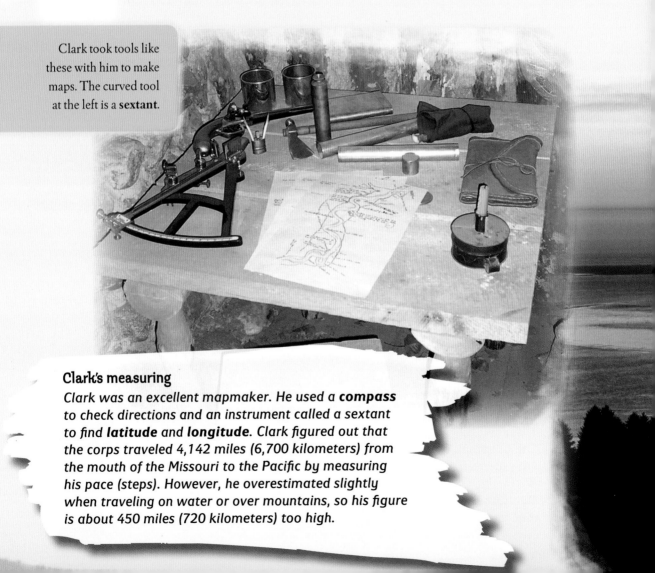

Clark took tools like these with him to make maps. The curved tool at the left is a **sextant**.

### Clark's measuring

*Clark was an excellent mapmaker. He used a **compass** to check directions and an instrument called a sextant to find **latitude** and **longitude**. Clark figured out that the corps traveled 4,142 miles (6,700 kilometers) from the mouth of the Missouri to the Pacific by measuring his pace (steps). However, he overestimated slightly when traveling on water or over mountains, so his figure is about 450 miles (720 kilometers) too high.*

When the men camped on the riverbank, Native Americans often visited. They were eager to trade for food, but Lewis and Clark had few supplies left. Whenever the river got wild, natives gathered on the shore to watch the corps struggle. They were ready to recover the supplies if the white men drowned.

## Is it the ocean?

On November 7, 1805, Clark thought he saw the Pacific Ocean. But it was not really the ocean. What Clark saw was the Columbia **estuary**. The men were trapped there for more than a week by high tides, wind, and bad weather. Everything and everyone was soaked. They had trouble starting fires because the wood was so wet.

### Estuary

*An estuary is a stretch of water that lies between a river and an ocean or sea. It is the area where the ocean tide meets the river current. High waves are common in an estuary. The expedition had to cross the Columbia estuary before it reached the Pacific.*

This bridge crosses the Columbia Estuary between Astoria, Oregon, and Meglar, Washington. It was completed in 1966 and is the longest bridge of its kind in the world.

## The Pacific, at last!

On November 14, 1805, Lewis led a small group to see the Pacific Ocean. He hoped to find a **trading post** or a ship there. Jefferson had wanted Lewis to bring the expedition home by ship. But there was no trading post. There were no ships.

Lewis carved his initials on a tree to show he had reached the ocean. Then, he returned to where Clark and the others waited. Clark went back to the tree where Lewis had carved his initials and added, "By land from the U. States in 1804 & 1805."

## Winter camp

On November 24 the captains asked the corps to vote on where to spend the winter. They could stay where they were, go back upriver, or cross the estuary to see if the land was better for camping there. Everyone voted—even York, a slave, and Sacagawea, a woman. It was a first in the history of the United States. They chose to stay where they were.

The corps spent December building a winter camp. They called it Fort Clatsop, after the local Clatsop people. They built a smokehouse to preserve meat. The only animal worth hunting was the elk. The men ate elk morning, noon, and night.

Constant rain rotted Fort Clatsop in the years after the expedition left. It was rebuilt in 1955 and is now run by the National Park Service.

## Smoking meat

*In the days before refrigerators, hunters preserved meat by smoking it. They cut the meat into strips and then hung it on wooden racks. They burned wet wood to make smoke. The smoke not only dried the meat, but also prevented **bacteria** from growing. This meant the meat was safe to eat. The dried meat had a smoky flavor.*

The Fort Clatsop storeroom had racks for drying meat as well as buckets for water, salt, and other supplies.

## Making salt

In addition to the smokehouse, the corps set up a salt works 15 miles (24 kilometers) south of Fort Clatsop. Salting is another way of preserving meat. The men built a furnace and boiled five kettles of salty ocean water for 24 hours a day. As the water boiled away, a fine layer of salt remained. They scraped off the salt, refilled the kettles, and began again. Between December and February, they produced 28 gallons (106 liters) of salt.

# Heading Home

It rained all winter at Fort Clatsop. The men were always wet and often sick with colds and flu. They were ready to go home. Clatsops visited daily and sold them furs. The men used these to make clothes and shoes in which to travel.

## The Clatsops

There were 300 to 400 members of the Clatsop tribe living at the mouth of the Columbia River when Lewis and Clark arrived. Clatsops were fishing people who lived in wooden houses. They had been traders since the early 1500s, when Europeans first visited the Oregon coast on their voyages of exploration up the west coast of North America.

## A dreaded journey

Lewis was especially eager to head home. He was worried about the dangerous trip over the mountains. After all, the **corps** had nearly starved on the way west. The expedition's hunters feared that food would also be hard to find on the trip east. The captains wondered whether they should wait until the salmon returned to the river in early May. But they decided to forge ahead. The corps left the coast on March 23, 1806.

## Dog thieves

On the night of April 11, three Clatsops stole Lewis' dog, Seaman. Lewis was running out of patience. He was tired, hungry, and eager to get home. He sent three soldiers to get the dog back, telling the men to shoot if the thieves did not give in. Luckily, when the thieves saw Lewis' men chasing them, they left the dog and ran off.

The captains traded Sacagawea's blue beads for a coat made of otter furs. Blue beads were highly prized among the Clatsops.

### Deadly smallpox

*In 1826 a **smallpox epidemic** nearly destroyed the Clatsops. Millions of Native Americans were killed by the disease. Smallpox is deadly and spreads quickly. Victims suffer from a high fever, headache, and backache, followed by an itchy rash. Smallpox was common in Europe from the 1500s. Spanish explorers brought it to the Americas in the early 1700s. In 1796 an English doctor named Edward Jenner discovered a **vaccine** to prevent smallpox. Today, the disease no longer exists.*

## Back across the Bitterroots

Lewis and Clark were relieved to reach the Nez Percé villages as they made their homeward journey. The villagers welcomed the expedition with dancing and games. Twisted Hair, the Nez Percé leader, warned the captains that snow blocked the Bitterroots. But Lewis and Clark were determined to move on.

The corps left the village on June 15 and discovered that there was no grass for the horses. Three days later, they found snow up to 10 feet (3 meters) deep. Lewis and Clark made the difficult decision to return to the village. On June 24 they started out again, this time with local guides. The snow was still deep, but the corps covered the 156 miles (251 kilometers) of mountain trails in six days.

This photo shows the Clark Fork River (named after William Clark) winding through the Bitterroot Mountains near present-day St. Regis, Montana.

### The Rocky Mountains

*The Rocky Mountains, often called the Rockies for short, stretch for 3,200 miles (5,100 kilometers) from Canada to New Mexico. Mount Elbert in Colorado is the highest peak, at 14,431 feet (4,399 meters). Many rivers, including the Colorado and the Yellowstone, have their source (starting point) in the Rocky Mountains. Lewis and Clark's path took them through the Bitterroot Range of the Rockies (see page 26).*

## Splitting up

Once they had crossed the mountains, Lewis and Clark decided to split up so they could explore more land. Clark took one group, including York, Charbonneau, Sacagawea, and Pomp. They headed for the Yellowstone River and sailed down it in two dugout canoes. When they reached the **prairies**, they saw huge herds of bison. They were excited at the sight of all that food.

Lewis and Clark split up on the return journey so that they could explore more of the area.

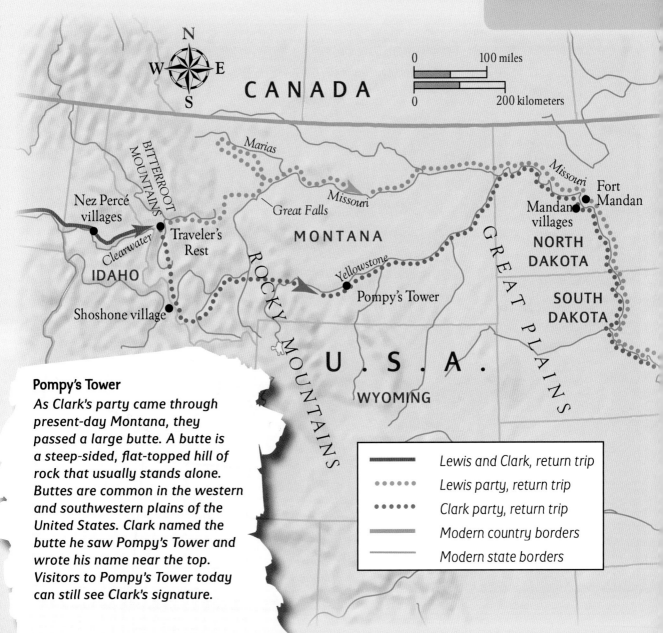

**Pompy's Tower**

*As Clark's party came through present-day Montana, they passed a large butte. A butte is a steep-sided, flat-topped hill of rock that usually stands alone. Buttes are common in the western and southwestern plains of the United States. Clark named the butte he saw Pompy's Tower and wrote his name near the top. Visitors to Pompy's Tower today can still see Clark's signature.*

| | |
|---|---|
| ▬▬▬▬ | *Lewis and Clark, return trip* |
| •••••• | *Lewis party, return trip* |
| •••••• | *Clark party, return trip* |
| ▬▬▬▬ | *Modern country borders* |
| ▬▬▬▬ | *Modern state borders* |

## Lewis and the Blackfeet

While Clark and his men sailed the Yellowstone, Lewis went in search of the Blackfeet people. He knew they were enemies of the Shoshone and Nez Percé, and he hoped to bring peace to the warring tribes. Lewis met with eight Blackfeet warriors. He told them that the United States would give them guns and supplies if they agreed to make peace.

The Blackfeet thought Lewis was threatening them. On the morning of July 27 several young Blackfeet warriors stole the corps' horses and guns. Lewis and his men fought for their belongings. In the battle, two of the Blackfeet died. Lewis and his men feared that they would be killed in revenge, so they rode for 20 hours without stopping to sleep. The Blackfeet did not follow.

U.S. artist George Catlin, a keen observer of Native Americans, painted this portrait of a Blackfoot chief in 1832.

## Stumbling on

Lewis and his men finally arrived at the Missouri and headed east, hunting elk on the way. On August 11 Lewis felt a bullet tear into his leg. One of his friends had shot him by mistake. In pain, Lewis made it back to the river and his **pirogue**. Just as he arrived, Clark's men appeared.

The two groups were happy to meet again, but Clark was concerned about Lewis. He hurried everyone on to the Mandan villages. They arrived on August 14. For Charbonneau, Sacagawea, and Pomp, this was the end of the journey. They were home.

## Pomp after the expedition

When Pomp was about five years old, his parents brought him to St. Louis. They lived there for about a year before Sacagawea and Charbonneau returned to the West with a fur-trading expedition. Pomp stayed with Clark, who treated him like a son. In 1812 Clark officially adopted Pomp and gave him a good education. Pomp traveled the world and was a friend to kings and princes. However, he always felt most at home in the wilderness.

Mandan villages were made of round earth lodges like the ones in this 1833 George Catlin painting.

### Mandan and Hidatsa today

*In 1837 smallpox broke out among the Mandan, killing most of the tribe. The survivors joined the Hidatsa at Like-a-Fishhook Village on the Missouri River. A third tribe, the Arikara, joined the Mandan and Hidatsa. In 1851 the U.S. government set up a reservation for these "Three Affiliated Tribes" at Fort Berthold in North Dakota. Today, about 3,800 tribe members live there. Another 8,000 live off the reservation.*

# Heroes of the Nation

Lewis recovered from his bullet wound in a few days. On August 17, 1806, the **corps** said goodbye to the Charbonneau family and raced back along the river toward St. Louis.

## Welcome home

The men traveled over 40 miles (more than 64 kilometers) most days down the Missouri. In just a little over a month, they reached white **settlements** along the river. People cheered and told the captains that all of the country feared they were dead. On September 23, 1806, the men reached St. Louis. Clark wrote in his journal, "We were met by all the village and received a hearty welcome from its inhabitants."

**Corps discoveries**

*The Corps of Discovery described 178 plants and 122 animals unknown to eastern U.S. scientists. They crossed land where hundreds of thousands of Native Americans lived. More than 50 tribes allowed the expedition to pass through their land; many of those offered food, shelter, and helpful information.*

People lined the river to greet the returning explorers. In this painting Lewis' dog, Seaman, jumps for shore.

## Rewards

Meriwether Lewis and William Clark became national heroes. Parties, dinners, and receptions were held in their honor. Jefferson rewarded each captain with 1,600 acres (about 650 hectares) of land and an important position. Lewis was made governor of the Louisiana **Territory** in 1807. Clark, who became superintendent of Indian affairs, continued working to help the Native Americans. In 1813 he became governor of the Missouri Territory.

This page from Clark's journal shows his detailed notes as well as his drawing of a sage grouse, which he called the Cock of the Plains.

### The journals

*Six members of the expedition kept journals. Patrick Gass published his in 1807. It included his drawings. In 1814 a short version of Lewis and Clark's journals was published. Then, in 2001, Gary Moulton of the University of Nebraska collected all the writings from the expedition into a 13-volume set. People can now read them online.*

# Lewis and Clark's Journey

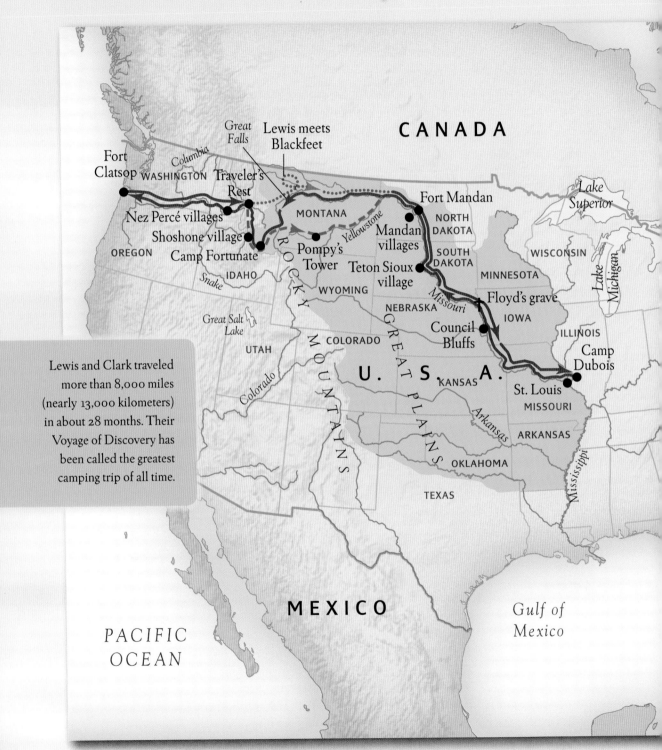

Lewis and Clark traveled more than 8,000 miles (nearly 13,000 kilometers) in about 28 months. Their Voyage of Discovery has been called the greatest camping trip of all time.

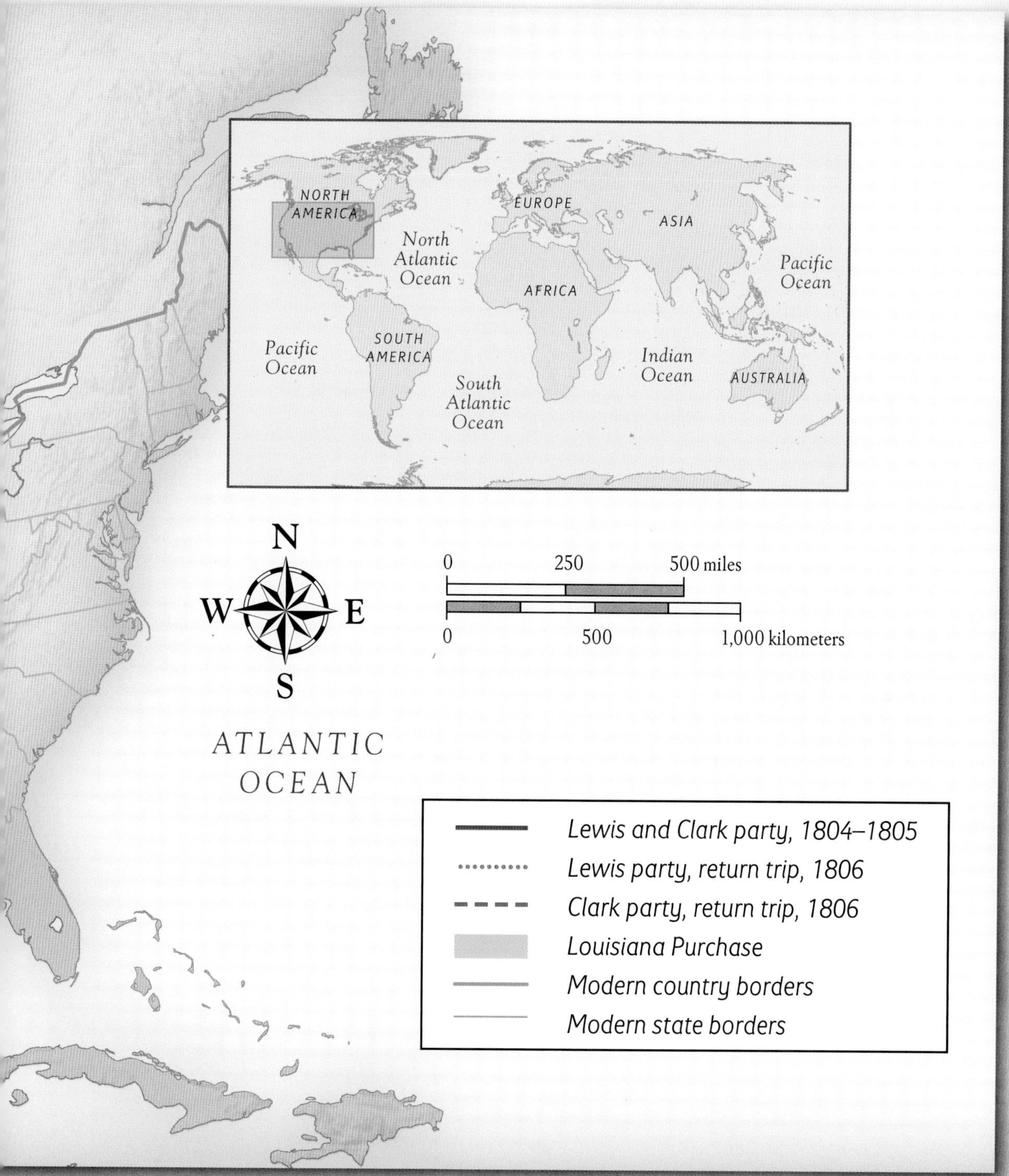

NORTH AMERICA
EUROPE
ASIA
North Atlantic Ocean
AFRICA
Pacific Ocean
SOUTH AMERICA
Pacific Ocean
Indian Ocean
AUSTRALIA
South Atlantic Ocean
N
W
E
S
0
250
500 miles
0
500
1,000 kilometers
ATLANTIC OCEAN
Lewis and Clark party, 1804–1805
Lewis party, return trip, 1806
Clark party, return trip, 1806
Louisiana Purchase
Modern country borders
Modern state borders

# Timeline

| | |
|---|---|
| **August 1, 1770** | William Clark is born in Virginia. |
| **August 18, 1774** | Meriwether Lewis is born in Virginia. |
| **1795** | Lewis and Clark meet while serving as soldiers on the United States **frontier.** |
| **1801** | Thomas Jefferson becomes president of the United States. Jefferson chooses Meriwether Lewis to be his secretary. |
| **1802–1804** | Jefferson and Lewis plan the Voyage of Discovery. |
| **January 18, 1803** | Jefferson requests Congress to approve the expedition and to provide $2,500 to pay for it. |
| **April 30, 1803** | The Louisiana Purchase: France sells the United States the Louisiana **Territory.** |
| **May 14, 1804** | The **Corps** of Discovery leaves St. Louis. |
| **August 3, 1804** | The first official meeting between Lewis and Clark and Native Americans takes place. |
| **September 25, 1804** | Lewis and Clark encounter the Teton Sioux. |
| **October 24, 1804** | The expedition arrives at the Mandan villages. |
| **November 4, 1804** | Lewis and Clark hire Toussaint Charbonneau and Sacagawea. |
| **December 24, 1804** | Fort Mandan is completed; the men move into the fort for winter. |
| **February 11, 1805** | Sacagawea's son, Pomp, is born. |
| **April 7, 1805** | The corps leaves Fort Mandan for the Pacific. |
| **June 13, 1805** | Lewis reaches the Great Falls. The corps spends the next two weeks hauling supplies around the waterfalls. |
| **July 22, 1805** | The expedition reaches Shoshone territory. |
| **August 17, 1805** | Sacagawea meets her brother, Cameahwait. |
| **August 31, 1805** | The corps leaves Shoshone country with Old Toby as a guide. |

| | |
|---|---|
| **September 11, 1805** | The corps begins to climb into the Bitterroot Mountains. |
| **September 22, 1805** | The corps arrives at the Nez Percé village, close to starvation. |
| **October 7, 1805** | The corps travels down the Clearwater River toward the Snake and Columbia rivers. |
| **November 7, 1805** | Clark sees the Columbia **estuary**; he thinks it is the Pacific. |
| **November 24, 1805** | The corps votes on where to spend winter. |
| **December 25, 1805** | The corps moves into Fort Clatsop and celebrates Christmas. |
| **March 23, 1806** | The corps leaves Fort Clatsop and begins the journey home. |
| **April 11, 1806** | Native Americans steal Seaman. The dog is eventually returned. |
| **May–June 1806** | The expedition reaches the Nez Percé village and waits for the snow to melt. |
| **June 15, 1806** | The corps begins crossing the Bitterroots. |
| **June 18, 1806** | Snow forces the corps to return to the Nez Percé village. |
| **June 24, 1806** | The corps sets off into the mountains again. |
| **June 30, 1806** | The corps completes the mountain crossing and re-enters the Great Plains. |
| **July 26, 1806** | Lewis meets Blackfeet warriors and kills two of them. |
| **August 14, 1806** | The corps reaches the Mandan villages. |
| **August 17, 1806** | The corps leaves the Charbonneaus and heads for St. Louis. |
| **September 23, 1806** | The corps arrives at St. Louis. |
| **1807** | Patrick Gass publishes his journal. |
| **October 11, 1809** | Meriwether Lewis dies. |
| **December 20, 1812** | Sacagawea dies. Soon after, Clark adopts her son, Pomp. |
| **September 1, 1838** | William Clark dies. |

# Glossary

**ammunition** bullets, gunpowder, cannonballs, or anything else that can be shot from a gun

**appendicitis** infection of the appendix, a small growth on the intestine. If untreated, appendicitis can kill.

**bacteria** microscopic organism (living thing). Some bacteria cause diseases if they get into the body—for example, by being swallowed in food.

**compass** instrument used to find directions. A compass has a magnetic needle that swings freely so that it always points to the north.

**continental climate** weather marked by extreme cold in winter and extreme heat in summer. The Mandan villages had a continental climate.

**Continental Divide** invisible line separating the east side from the west side of a continent

**corps** group of people (often military) working together toward a certain goal

**dam** barrier that holds back water. There are now several dams on the Missouri and Columbia rivers. Many of these are used for hydroelectric power.

**epidemic** any disease that spreads rapidly through a community. Smallpox epidemics killed entire Native American tribes during the 1800s.

**estuary** body of water that lies between a river and an ocean

**frontier** unsettled area of a country

**frostbite** injury caused by extreme cold. Skin of the ears, fingers, and toes may suffer from frostbite if exposed to freezing temperatures.

**hydroelectric power** electricity produced using the power of running water

**keelboat** large boat that can be pushed, rowed, or pulled

**landmark** prominent feature of the landscape

**latitude** distance measured in degrees north or south of the Equator

**longitude** distance measured in degrees east or west of an imaginary line called the prime meridian, which runs through Greenwich, England

**medicinal herb** plant used to cure various illnesses

**omnivore** animal that eats both plants and animals. Bears are omnivores.

**peace pipe** decorated pipe smoked at ceremonies, especially as a sign of peace

**pirogue** canoe made from a hollowed-out log. The pirogues that the expedition used were large enough to hold several people.

**pollution** anything that dirties or harms water, air, or land. There was very little pollution when Lewis and Clark crossed North America.

**portage** carrying boats or supplies overland between or around bodies of water

**prairie** natural grassland, also known as plain. Herds of bison, pronghorn antelope, and many other animals make the prairies their home.

**Revolutionary War** (1775–1783) war that brought the United States independence from England

**settlement** place where people live

**sextant** instrument used to measure the distance between the Sun, Moon or stars, and the horizon

**smallpox** infectious disease with fever, vomiting, and marks on the skin. Many adults who survived smallpox were left with scars on their faces and bodies from the disease.

**territory** area under control of a nation or country. Jefferson purchased the Louisiana Territory.

**trading post** store on the frontier where goods were exchanged with natives. English and French traders stopped at trading posts throughout the prairies to buy furs.

**vaccine** preparation that gives someone protection from a disease. The vaccine for smallpox came too late to save many Native Americans.

# Further Information

## Books

Blue, Rose, and Corinne J. Naden. *Exploring the Pacific Northwest*. Chicago: Raintree, 2003. Examine the journeys through the Pacific Northwest made by explorers such as Lewis and Clark and Zebulon Pike.

Nelson, Sheila. *Thomas Jefferson's America: The Louisiana Purchase 1800–1811*. Philadelphia: Mason Crest, 2005. An examination of Thomas Jefferson's presidency, with a focus on how the nation greatly expanded during this period with the Louisiana Purchase.

Patent, Dorothy Hinshaw. *Animals on the Trail with Lewis and Clark*. New York: Clarion, 2002. Learn about the wildlife the Corps of Discovery encountered, including buffaloes, coyotes, grizzly bears, and more.

Patent, Dorothy Hinshaw. *Plants on the Trail with Lewis and Clark*. New York: Clarion, 2003. Learn about the various plants the Corps of Discovery encountered.

## Websites

www.sierraclub.org/lewisandclark/
Follow in the footsteps of Lewis and Clark with the Sierra Club.

www.pbs.org/lewisandclark/index.html
Learn more about Lewis and Clark at PBS.

http://libtextcenter.unl.edu/lewisandclark/index.html
Read the journals of the expedition.

## Places to Visit

Lewis and Clark National Historical Park
Astoria, Oregon
Phone: (503) 861-2471 ext. 214
Website: www.nps.gov/lewi/

A collection of 12 different sites, operated by the National Park Service, within a 40-mile stretch of the Pacific Coast. These include a reconstructed Fort Clatsop, the Salt Works, and an Interpretive Center at Cape Disappointment. Park rangers and displays explain Lewis and Clark's West Coast experiences.

Museum of Westward Expansion
St. Louis, Missouri
Phone: (314) 655-1700
Website: www.nps.gov/jeff/planyourvisit/museum-of-westward-expansion.htm

Museum displays include rare items from the Lewis and Clark expedition. There are Jefferson peace medals, maps, and a full-size Native American tepee (tent). A theater shows a film about the expedition. Other exhibits focus on the Louisiana Purchase and pioneer journeys West.

North Dakota Lewis & Clark Interpretive Center
Washburn, North Dakota
Phone: (877) 462-8535
Website: www.fortmandan.com

Visit the reconstructed Fort Mandan to see how Lewis and Clark spent the winter of 1805. Displays include a buffalo robe that visitors can try on, Native American artifacts, and an authentic canoe like those used by Lewis and Clark. An art gallery features watercolor paintings of Native American life and culture by artist Karl Bodmer.

# Index